THE VOW

For my Brothers and Sisters
of the Society of St. Francis:
my friends, teachers and companions

THE VOWS BOOK

Anglican Teaching
on the Vows of
Obedience, Poverty and Chastity

Clark Berge,
Society of St. Francis

Vest Pocket Publications
Mt. Sinai, NY

Copyright @ 2014 by The Society of St. Francis

All right reserved. No part of this book may be reproduced or transmitted in any form or by any means, electronic or mechanical, including photocopying, recording, or any information storage and retrieval system, without acknowledgement of the author, except in the case of brief quotations embodied in critical articles and reviews.

Berge, Clark, 1958-.
The Vows Book : Anglican teaching on the vows of obedience, poverty, and chastity / Clark Berge, Society of St. Francis.

Unless otherwise noted, scripture quotations are from the Good News Translation, revised edition, @ American Bible Society 1966, 1971, 1976, 1992.

Published by Vest Pocket Publications
Box 399, Mt. Sinai, NY 11766

The cover art by Clark Berge is a meditation on Baptism, inspired by the words of Ephrem the Syrian (Ephrem of Nisibis, died June 9, 373, Edessa, Turkey):
"Behold: Fire and Spirit in the womb that bore you:
Behold: Fire and Spirit in the river where you were baptized."

Editor—V.K. McCarty
Book and Cover design—Melinda Kwok

Printed in the United States of America by Mission Graphics,
Episcopal Church of Our Savior

ISBN 978-1495378812

Light-seeds are planted in the souls of God's people,
Joy-seeds are planted in good heart-soil.

Psalm 97:11
The Message (MSG)

Table of Contents

Foreword	9
Acknowledgements	11
Chapter 1: Basic Background	15
Part 1: Vowed Religious are part of the Anglican Communion	17
Part 2: The vowed life starts in Baptism	27
Part 3: The vowed life is about going into the heart of the world	33
Chapter 2: Obedience	43
Part 1: Obedience means listening	43
Part 2: Obedience means listening to the Bible	47
Part 3: Obedience means listening to our Founders	51
Part 4: Obedience means listening to Each Other	55
Part 5: Obedience means listening to our Inner Voices	61
Part 6: Obedience means listening to Nature	65

Chapter 3: Poverty ... 72

    Part 1: Poverty means following the example of Jesus ... 72

    Part 2: Religious Poverty is freely chosen ... 80

    Part 3: Religious Poverty helps us help the poor ... 83

    Part 4: Religious Poverty makes our social vision clear ... 88

Chapter 4: Chastity ... 93

    Part 1: What do we mean by chastity and celibacy? ... 93

    Part 2: What are some good reasons for taking the vow of chastity? ... 99

    Part 3: What about sexy thoughts and feelings? ... 104

    Part 4: How does chastity help us tell out the Good News? ... 110

Chapter 5: Living the vows and prayer ... 115

Chapter 6: Putting it all together ... 123

Appendix ... 130

Foreword

Max Lucado in *The Applause of Heaven* attests to the passion God has for all creation.

> Blessed are the available –
> Blessed are the conduits,
> the tunnels, the tools.
> Deliriously joyful are
> the Ones who believe –
> that if God has used
> sticks and rocks to do God's will –
> then God can use us. [1]

Some cynics describe the vows of poverty, chastity and obedience as "no dough, no sex, no say." The religious life is a powerful expression of Christ-like availability. The discipline of prayer that flows into a fragile community of brothers and sisters seeking to live out the demands of the Gospel is worthy of the applause of heaven.

The Psalmist describes an amazing truth, "Awake my soul, awake lute and harp: for I will awaken the morning." (58:9) – silence, prayer and praise give birth to the dawn – awaken promise, possibility and prophetic endeavour.

In *The Vows Book: Anglican Teaching on the Vows of Obedience, Poverty and Chastity*, Br. Clark Berge, SSF offers a well-spring – fresh, inviting, simple, joyful, demanding – grounded in trembling, real temptations and trials. Exuberant joy and agonising pain accompany the response to the awesome divine initiative.

Written from a lived experience of seeking to keep "the vows" and attentive to many of the religious for whom English is a third or fourth language, this book comes alive through its acknowledgement of imperfection in the individuals and communities who seek to live "the vows."

I hope that this resource with its inductive, invitational and challenging style will be welcomed by religious communities, by all the baptised and by those who are seeking to hear God's "yes" in our world.

> You dare your Yes and experience a meaning. You repeat your Yes and all things acquire meaning. When everything has meaning, how can you live anything but a Yes. For all that has been – Thanks. To all that shall be – Yes.
>
> Dag Hammarskjöld, *Markings*. [2]

May the vows we make be held in the great vow of God to us in Christ – "Yes."

> For in him every one of God's promises is a 'Yes.' For this reason it is through him that we say the 'Amen' to the glory of God. (2 Corinthians 1:20)
>
> The Most Reverend Roger Herft AM
> Archbishop of Perth
> Protector General, Society of St. Francis

Acknowledgements

My first, and deepest, thanks go to my brothers and sisters of the Society of St. Francis, particularly the brothers I have lived with over the years. I got the ideas for this book from thinking about, and praying about, our life together. My first mentor was Br. Jon Bankert SSF, who died in 2007. His wry, loving spirit still guides and provokes me.

There have been many others who have given me tremendous support and help in my vocation. One of the earliest, and still today, is Barbara S. Bates who listened to me as a young man, supported me for ordination and has never given up her challenge to me to write.

In writing this book, I have received a lot of help and good feedback. Especially I thank Br. Jude Hill SSF, Dr. Petà Dunstan, and the Rev. Barbara Crafton, the first ones to read a draft and respond to it. Brothers Luke Manitara SSF, Matthew Sikoboki SSF, Wilbert SSF and Simone Schiaratura SSF, read through the book with me at the Stroud Spirituality Programme in Australia. Hearing them read the book and our conversations about it, their questions and comments, were invaluable. Thanks also to other readers and their thoughtful responses: Susan Pitchford, the Rev. Richard Carter, the Rev. Pirrial Clift, the Rev. Roger Sharr, Suzanne Lawson, David Richo, Hannah Fields, Br. Samuel SSF, Br. Michael Lapsely SSM, Br. John Forbes OHC, Br. Daniel Ludik OHC, Br. Thomas Carey SSF, Br. Simon SSF, Sr. Pamela Clare CSF.

I have been blessed by the response and support I have received from Archbishop Roger Herft. I am grateful for his nurturing care and extraordinary Gospel vision as he cares for the world-wide Society of St. Francis, in all three orders.

A hearty thanks to the Trustees of the Legacy Fund of the Society of St. Francis whose support and confidence in this project made it possible.

In getting the book ready for publication my very special thanks to V.K. McCarty who devoted so much time to editing the book, checking references and giving me advice on a host of matters. Her humor, passion for religious life and humility as she read and commented on the text has inspired me.

With a full heart I acknowledge and give God praise for my father and mother, brother and sisters and their spouses who gave me my first experiences of community and the lessons of listening, trusting and loving.

Before you start to read this book

This book about the vows is written in long thin columns so that they are easy to read and understand after the way of a Roman Catholic writer named Peter Maurin, who wrote "Easy Essays" on different topics. Maurin wrote during the middle of the twentieth century in America. His writing and ideas were very important for the Catholic Worker Movement, a group of people who lived together and worked with poor people. He wrote so that everybody could understand what he was trying to say, to inspire them to act for social justice. What he says about religious orders in the Catholic Church fits religious orders in the Anglican Communion. I think it is very important that brothers and sisters understand what the vows mean. If we have a good idea about them, it will help us to live them with happiness and to serve God and people better; to become as Peter Maurin says, a "dominant social dynamic force in our day and age." Here is an example of one of his Easy Essays:

A New Society
by Peter Maurin

To be radically right
is to go to the roots
by fostering a society
based on a creed,
systematic unselfishness
and gentle personalism.
To foster a society
based on creed
instead of greed,
on systematic unselfishness
instead of systematic selfishness,

on gentle personalism
instead of rugged individualism,
is to create a new society
within the shell of the old.
Modern society
is in a state of chaos.
And what is chaos
if not lack of order?
Sociology
is not a science,
it is an art,
the art of creating order
out of chaos.
All founders of orders
made it their personal business
to try to solve the problems
of their own day.
If religious orders
made it their business
to try to solve the problems
of our own day
by creating order
out of chaos,
the Catholic Church
would be the dominant
social dynamic force
in our day and age.
—*Easy Essays* [3]

Chapter 1: Basic Background

To teach about the vows
is to tell a story
about the Holy Spirit.

The Holy Spirit
calls us,
moves us,
helps us
to be brothers and sisters
in religious orders.

But the Holy Spirit
never forces us.
We are called, not pushed.
Everything
happens
in freedom.

To profess the vowed life
is to step through
a gate,
to set out
on a journey
led by the Spirit.
As one brother says:
"We go looking for trouble.
We go looking to be disturbed.
We go to change the world." [4]

What do the vows
mean to you?

I hope you find
this book
a way
to step out

onto Jesus' Way,
to discover
the vows
and experience
the joy of them
in your heart.

In this first chapter
of the book,
there are three parts where
I talk about
three important things
to get us ready
to study the vows
of obedience,
poverty,
and chastity.
The first is learning
that vowed religious
are part of the
Anglican Communion.

The second key teaching is that
vowed life
starts in Baptism.

The third teaching
is about how joining a religious order
and taking vows
means we are going
into the heart
of the world.

Part 1:
Vowed Religious are Part of the Anglican Communion

This is a short history,
to help you know how we started.
There are not very many Anglican religious
in the world today.
Most people don't know
the Anglican Communion has religious orders.
There are just over 8,000
religious
of one kind or another.

There are about 2,000
traditional vowed religious
in the Anglican Communion.
"Traditional"
means men and women who take vows
and live
in community
without a wife or husband—they are called "celibate."
I will talk more about
celibacy
when we study
chastity
later in this book.
There are over
3,000 Third Order Society of St. Francis
and another 3,000
non-celibate religious
in different communities,
meaning those brothers or sisters
can also
be married.

There aren't very many teachings
in the Anglican Churches

about vows and religious orders.
Because
for much of our history as Anglicans
there were no religious orders.

Then the Holy Spirit started something.

In the 1800's,
there was a movement for change
in the Anglican Church,
the Oxford Movement.
This movement was started in Oxford, England in 1833.
The people wanted
to find again
Catholic teaching and spirituality
for the Anglican Church.
Catholic teaching and spirituality
means
they wanted to live like Christians
in the first centuries
after Jesus lived.
The Acts of the Apostles
gives us a picture
of what they wanted:
"All the believers
continued together
in close fellowship
and shared their belongings
with one another.
They would sell
their property and possessions,
and distribute the money
among all, according
to what each one needed." (Acts 2:44-45)

They wanted
to help the poor,
to help children with no parents,
to build schools,
hospitals.

They wanted
to keep the Church special,
free from government control,
because it is founded by God
and is the Body of Christ.
They wanted
Holy Communion
every day, if possible,
using candles and vestments;
they wanted to remember
and celebrate
the special days for saints.
They wanted religious orders
to carry on
the work and message
of the saints,
like St. Benedict and St. Francis and St. Clare.
And they wanted to make
more saints,
meaning they wanted to help
more people to be
holy people,
to show
God's love and power in the world.

It was a woman
who first responded to the call
to live as an
Anglican religious:
Marian Rebecca Hughes
took her vows in 1841 in Oxford.
Later in 1849,
she founded a community,
The Society of the Holy and Undivided Trinity.
But the first community for women
was The Sisterhood of the Holy Cross.
It was founded by Emma Langston,
in London in 1845.

Father Richard Meux Benson
was the first man
to respond and stay,
answering God's call
to start a religious order for men,
one that still exists today
in the Anglican Communion.
In 1866 he founded
The Society of St. John the Evangelist
at Cowley, Oxford, England.
They are called the Cowley Fathers
in England and America.

The traditional orders
in the Anglican Communion today
number 13 communities for men,
57 communities for women,
and 7 communities for men and women together.[5]
Some religious live in community houses,
some live separately, on their own.

Most religious take vows
of obedience, poverty and chastity.
You can keep these vows
wherever you go.
For example,
Franciscan brothers and sisters
who go out to preach in churches
and work in the community
or travel a lot in their ministry
keep these vows.
Other religious orders
were started by different people.
Each community's way of life
is a little bit different.
For example,
those who follow the example of St. Benedict
take different vows:
obedience, stability and conversion of life.

They promise not to marry, too.
It is very important for them
that they live in one place
for most of their life.
But all of the brothers and sisters in religious orders
want to give their lives to God
in a special way.

Even though Anglican religious
are a small part of the Church,
being small
can be a good thing.
It is easier to know
and to pray for each other
in small communities.
In my community,
The Society of St. Francis,
we pray for each other
by name
all year round.

Also, it is easier to change things
or try new things
with a smaller group of people.
An Anglican woman
and famous anthropologist
who studied different human cultures,
Margaret Mead,
once said:
"Never doubt that a small group
of people
can change the world:
it's all that ever has." [6]
And Jesus teaches us
big things can come out of
little mustard seeds.

Our life of prayer
and service

makes us radical.
We have an important
part to play
in the Anglican Communion.

In 1878
in Memphis, Tennessee
in the United States of America
the sisters of
an Episcopal religious order,
(The Episcopal Church
is part of the Anglican Communion
in the USA),
The Sisters of the
Community of St. Mary,
took care of people sick
with yellow fever,
a deadly disease.
Everybody else ran away.
In the end,
the sisters and others died. [7]

Here's another story
from not so long ago:

From 1999 until 2004
the four religious orders
in the Anglican Church of Melanesia,
The Society of St. Francis,
The Sisters of the Church,
The Melanesian Brotherhood,
The Sisters of Melanesia,
worked to bring peace
to their country,
The Solomon Islands.
A violent ethnic conflict
was hurting the country.

Their gift
to the peace process
was their commitment
to prayer,
their knowledge of God's love
for themselves and all people.
Their "no" to hate,
their "yes" to love,
made all the difference.
From time to time
the religious
could cross ethnic dividing lines
with food, medicine
and they could pass messages to worried families
about loved ones.
They refused
to take sides
and promised to help
everybody in need.
It was very dangerous work.

In 2003,
seven members of
the Melanesian Brotherhood
were kidnapped by militants
in the ethnic conflict.
On August 8, 2003
the community got the news,
the terrible news,
of their deaths.
Beaten,
tortured,
brutally murdered:
Robin Lindsay,
Francis Tofi,
Alfred Hill,
Ini Paratobatu,
Patteson Gatu,
Tony Sirihi,
Nathaniel Sado.

In his book,
In Search of the Lost
Richard Carter,
priest,
chaplain to the brothers,
then for a time a brother, too,
writes:
"Of one thing
I am certain:
these seven men
will live on
in the hearts and minds
of the Community.
Their sacrifice seems
too great and hard
to believe...
these young men
believed in peace
and goodness.
They knew that there was
a better way.
They were prepared
to oppose violence
and to risk much.
At the end of the day
they stand against
all acts
of brutality
which are at present
disfiguring our world,
and bravely,
boldly,
and with love
lived
what most of us
proclaim only
from the safety of a church.
Oh, how much
the world-wide Anglican Church
at the moment

could learn from
their witness!
And when such
real-life issues
are so much at stake
in our world,
is not this
what the gospel
should be?" [8]

Christians,
and maybe members of religious orders most of all,
call it joy
when we serve Christ
in the poor,
the sick,
the outcast,
not counting the cost,
knowing, like St. Paul,
"All this I do
for the Gospel's sake
in order to share in its
blessings." (1 Corinthians 9:23)

The Anglican Communion
can learn from the religious orders.
We teach from our experience
of praying every day,
from sharing everyday life,
being a brother or sister
to people from different
tribes, cultures, races.
We teach about community
because we live together
when we agree
and when we don't,
in sickness and in health,
for richer or poorer.
We can teach Anglicans
about peace and respect,

and to love each other,
and God.
In the words
of The General Thanksgiving:
...we show forth God's praise
not only with our lips
but with our lives,
by giving up ourselves
to God's service,
and by walking before God
in holiness and in righteousness
all our days..." [9]

God calls us
into community.
There we are helped
through our vows
to find deep Christian peace
for ourselves
and to bring
healing to our Church
and the world.
Because of our witness,
seeds get planted,
one way or another,
and men and women
start to wonder:
"What is God doing?"
For some,
"Is this for me?"
"Is God calling me to live with these people?"

Some things to think about and talk about

Tell the story about how you found out about religious life.

If you are thinking about joining a religious order,
what do you like about the idea?

If you are a member of a religious order,
tell somebody else
why you stay in the community.

How can you help more people find out
it is possible to live
this radical way of life
in the Anglican Communion?

Part 2:
The Vowed Life Starts in Baptism

Religious life starts
with water
splashing
over our heads:
Baptism.

Baptism makes us Christian.
We are anointed
by the Holy Spirit
and made part
of the Body of Christ.
He lives in us,
and we live in him.
It is a new deal
for humanity.
In some parts
of the Anglican Communion
in the new liturgies for Baptism
we make special vows:
1) to continue in the apostle's teaching and fellowship,
in breaking the bread,
and in the prayers...
2) to persevere in resisting evil,
and, whenever we fall into sin,
repent and return to the Lord...

3) to proclaim by word and example
the Good News of God in Christ...
4) to seek and serve Christ in all persons,
loving our neighbor
as our self...
5) to strive for justice and peace among all people,
and respect the dignity
of every human being... [10]

As we grow up
many of us wonder,
"How should I live out my Baptism?
What is the best way
to show Jesus Christ to the world?"

The best way to live out Baptism
is to live with Jesus
prayerfully,
joyfully,
gratefully.
It means
doing whatever we can
to help in the world—
something that gives us joy,
and makes the world
a better place.
This brings together
in Christ
our prayer,
our work,
our relationships,
all the things that are important to us.

Baptized people come together every week,
sometimes every day,
to share Holy Communion,
to read the Bible,
to experience God's love and forgiveness,
to encourage each other,

to stand together against evil,
to proclaim Jesus as our Savior.

We brothers and sisters
live out our Baptism by
joining a religious order.
Living out our Baptism
is the best reason we can give
for joining an order.
Baptism is serious business.
A friend once said to someone,
just before he joined an order:
"I have always thought it nice
that you liked church,
but I am very surprised
you take it so seriously."

To be serious
about church,
especially to join a religious order,
is to choose
to live
joyfully
a way of life
different
from our families
and our cultures.
Some parts of our cultures
we keep:
language, arts, food,
for example.
But some parts of religious life
don't fit any culture
very well.
Our vows make us very different
from our cultures
which teach us
to marry
and to make money,

whether we are from
"Western" culture
or "Asian,"
or any kind of native culture.
In joining a religious order
we choose
to put God first
and build a
community of Baptized people
who will live another way
deep in society.
Like a piece of sand
in an oyster shell,
we can cause
big problems for some people
because of our different
life and values.
And at the same time,
we make something
very valuable.
A pearl
of great price.

Baptismal vows and religious vows
are very close together.
They are all about
prayer, service and social justice.
Marriage vows also grow
out of Baptism,
as do Ordination vows.
It is the same Spirit
working in the hearts
of Christian people
to fulfill God's dream for humanity.
Different calls for different people.

For some of us
taking religious vows
is more like getting married

than getting ordained.
We are giving ourselves
to our community
and all the brothers or sisters
for better or worse,
for richer for poorer,
in sickness and in health,
until we die.
We all have different gifts
for ministry
that make the community happy
and its mission strong.
It is together
we make a difference
in society.

For Anglicans
the grace of ordination
has nothing to do
with marriage
or celibacy.
It is open to both kinds of Baptized people.
Still,
for many women,
religious life is also the best way
to have a ministry in the Church
because not all Anglican Churches
welcome ordained women.

And that is another book!

For this book,
the choice between getting married
and joining a traditional religious order
is about God's call to you.

If you are called
to be married,
it will fill your

mind and heart
and keep you restless
until it happens.
The Church teaches that
God made this way of life
for the shared joy
of living together and maybe raising children
and sharing in Christian life where you live.

If you are called
to be a religious,
it will fill your
mind and heart
and keep you restless
until it happens.
The Church teaches that
God made this way of life
for the shared joy
of living together and sharing
regular times of prayer and service,
sharing God's love
with everyone you meet.

Think what the world would look like
if every Christian
woke up to the possibilities
of Baptismal life.
Think about a world with no war,
no poverty,
happy families
and communities.

Some things to think about and talk about

Do you remember your Baptism?

Take some time to draw a picture about Baptism,
using colors if you have them.

Show the picture to somebody else
and talk about it with them.

What special meaning
does Baptism have for your Christian life?

Why did you decide to join a religious order?

If you are still finding out about religious orders
in the Anglican Communion,
why do you hope to join a religious order?

What did your friends and family say when you told them?

Part 3:
The Vowed Life is about Going into the Heart of the World

When I first began to think
about becoming a member
of a religious order
of Anglican Franciscans,
The Society of St. Francis,
I knew nothing,
about the vows of obedience,
poverty
and chastity.
I had only
read a book about St. Francis.
Still, that book made me think
I wanted to follow
the example of St. Francis.

Some people said they were sad
to see me leave the world
and join a religious order.
But leaving is not what I experienced

when I joined a religious order.
I jumped
straight into the heart of the world.
I learned to see the world
like a poor person.
I grew to understand
how much I need God.

I also had some secret
fears and hopes
that pushed me forward.

Fears?
I was scared about sex and relationships.
I thought if I took a vow of chastity
I would never need
to think about my sex problems
ever again.

But I learned
that is not how chastity works.

Hopes?
I wanted to live
a seriously Christian life
of prayer and service.
I wanted to take vows
and live—
—like St. Francis and St. Clare,
—like Ini Kopuria,
founder of the Anglican
Melanesian Brotherhood,
—like Bernard Mizeki,
an Anglican saint in Africa,
—like Mother Emily,
founder of the Anglican
Sisters of the Church.
I still hope to live like them,
to do something important

for Jesus Christ.
I am learning
"important" does not mean
front page of the newspaper,
but everyday faithfulness.

Of course,
religious life isn't for everybody.
But the same could be said
of any hard discipline:
playing music
studying science,
running a marathon.
These are not for everybody,
but they are
important, beautiful, valuable.
They are some of the things
that make life worth living.
And they require
a total way of life,
a change in thinking and acting.
All of these things
—as well as religious life—
add to our understanding
of what it means
to be a human being.
When I first joined,
I found out that by
taking vows of obedience,
poverty,
and chastity,
I could live
a faithful life,
a creative life,
a happy life.

Still, some people wonder (I did):
is this way of living
possible to do for a long time,

or even for a whole life?
Maybe you wonder, too.
It is a happy life,
but also very hard in some ways.

What is important to ask yourself is this:
Do I believe the Holy Spirit
wants me to serve God
as a brother
or sister
in a religious order?
If the answer is "yes,"
then it is important
to ask how the vows
can help you in your life and ministry.
Think of them
as special blessings;
as resources,
not burdens
in your life.

On a bad day,
I admit
the vows are bad news.
I think:
Obedience: NO thinking for myself! Follow the rules!
Poverty: NO money!
Chastity: NO sex!

NO! NO! NO!
When I think like that,
the vows
are heavy burdens
and I start looking
for ways to get out
from under it all.

"NO" is not helpful to us,
as we follow Jesus today.

Where is the Good News in "No"?
The vows are how we say "Yes"
to God.
They are our "Yes"
to the fullness of life.

There are many
chances
to go deeper,
learn more,
love more
in religious life.
For some of us,
we live together
because "the spirit is willing
but the flesh is weak,"
and we need
encouragement from each other.

If we tell the truth,
nobody lives the vows perfectly—
who lives any life
"perfectly?"
God knows
what we go through.
So, ask for help.
God sent Jesus
to be human
and share our life
and its struggles.
We are loved,
accepted
no matter what.
It is grace,
grace,
grace
all the way.
After living the vowed life
for a while,

I felt deep down
something wasn't right.
I had to jump again,
deeper into God's heart.
This second time
was harder.
I asked for help.
The brothers told me
what they thought
about my life,
good and bad.
I found I had to give
more of myself,
all of myself,
to Christ.
When we take vows,
we keep growing,
we keep seeking conversion.

I learned
I drank too much alcohol.
Drinking too much alcohol
is a disease like cancer.
I recognized myself
as one of the sick and suffering
of the world.
Not a hero,
but an ordinary man
who needs God's help.
I felt shame
when people said
I drank too much.
I tried
to explain it away:
"I only drink to have fun," I said.
"And when I am tired,
or lonely,
or feeling angry."
"Perhaps you need to learn more about fun,"

I was told.
How many drinks
does it take to have fun?
Why could I never remember?
Was feeling sick
fun?
Was lying about how I spent my money
fun?
My community held me tight.
They asked me to tell the truth.
I don't think
I have done anything
as painful
as telling these truths
about myself.

Because I wanted to feel alive,
free, happy and honest,
I looked at my life.
I told the truth
more and more
to myself and others.
I learned to pray for help
every time I wanted to drink.
I learned not to count
other people's sins.
(I always found other people's problems
good reasons to drink).
I learned not to tell God
what to do.
I learned to love
more and more.
I learned to serve other people
who suffered from the same problem,
helping them
to ask for God's help
to live without alcohol.
This work
is a big part of my life.

In my life as a brother
I have served in many ways.
I have been a leader
in The Society of St. Francis.
I have worked for social justice
in different places
around the world.
I could tell you lots of stories
about me,
but I only share
a few things
that maybe will help you
to look at your life.

God is looking for you and me
all the time.
God loves us
more than anything.
He can forgive us anything.
This God
wants our help.
He wants us to wake up
to follow the Holy Spirit.
God is calling you and me
on an adventure with Jesus.

As we begin to think
about the vows
the important questions are:
"Who am I?"
And "Who are you, Lord?"
The simple thing
is that we must tell the truth
as much as we can stand it.
And then more
when we are ready,
because the truth
will get us closer
to where we want to be.

At the heart of the world
is the heart of Jesus.

Some things to think about and talk about

What are some things you are afraid of,
or feel sorry about
when you think about your life?

Can you name them and ask for help?
Or give them to God in prayer?

If you are thinking about joining an order,
what strengths and weaknesses do you have to share
with the order?

What are the things
about being a brother or sister
that make you happy?

To Sum Up: Important Teachings to Remember from this Chapter

1. Anglican religious orders
   have served the church
   and the world in very important ways,
   like taking care of sick people and working for peace.
   We pray for courage to keep doing this work.
2. Religious brothers and sisters are called,
   like all baptized Christians,
   to live differently in the world.
   The Holy Spirit gives us gifts we need
   to live in religious communities.

3. The call to religious life takes us deeper into human life.
   Our religious commitment
   helps us live more and more honestly,
   depending on other brothers and sisters to help us.

Chapter 2: Obedience

When we join a religious order,
our first promise is obedience.
I want to talk about six different parts of the vow of obedience.

Part 1: Obedience means listening.
Part 2: Obedience means listening to the Bible.
Part 3: Obedience means listening to our founders.
Part 4: Obedience means listening to each other, leaders and members.
Part 5: Obedience means listening to our inner voice.
Part 6: Obedience means listening to nature.

Part 1:
Obedience Means Listening

This is a Bible story that teaches that listening
is an important part of obedience:

The Lord called Samuel.
He answered, "Yes, sir!" and ran to Eli and said,
"You called me, and here I am."
But Eli answered, "I didn't call you;
go back to bed."
So Samuel went back to bed.
The Lord called Samuel again.
The boy did not know that it was the Lord,
because the Lord had never spoken to him before.
So he got up, went to Eli,
and said,
"You called me, and here I am."
But Eli answered, "My son, I didn't call you;
go back to bed."
The Lord called Samuel a third time;
he got up, went to Eli, and said

"You called me, and here I am."
Then Eli realized it was the Lord
who was calling the boy,
so he said to him,
"Go back to bed; and if he calls you again, say,
'Speak, Lord, your servant is listening.'"
So Samuel went back to bed.
The Lord came and stood there, and called as he had before,
"Samuel! Samuel!"
Samuel answered, "Speak; your servant is listening."
(1 Samuel 3:4-10)

And then, as you know
the Lord gave Samuel a special message.

The religious understanding of obedience
is about listening.
You can look it up in the dictionary:
the Latin words that over time
became the English word "obedience"
were *ob audire*:
"to listen with full attention."
It is what we are supposed to do.
It is our response
when God calls us.

As a novice
I promised to be obedient
to the Rule of my religious order.
I thought perhaps that meant obedience only:
 "Don't worry about poverty or chastity yet!"
But I was wrong.
Poverty and chastity
are part of our Rule
I was promising to obey.
I was just a beginner
(that is what "novice" means);
what did I know?

I promised to do my best
to listen to the community's teachings,
to learn about the life of the community,
to find out if this life was good for me.
And to change my thinking
where it was selfish
or based on ideas like
"Be a winner,"
"Men don't cry,"
"I always know the right answer."

The thing about obedience
is that all Christians are called by the Holy Spirit
to live obediently:
to listen with full attention to the Gospels,
aiming to fulfill
the promises we made,
or those made for us by our parents and godparents
at our Baptism.
In religious orders
we take time,
to listen carefully.

Some people think to be obedient
means to do what you are told,
no questions asked.
We train dogs and horses
and even children
to be obedient.
"Come."
"Sit."
"Run."
"Be quiet."
"Do as you are told."
We reward them when they are good,
and punish them when they are bad.

It works with some pets
and some children for a time,

until they start asking "why?"
at around age two.

However, we are already raised,
by the time we think to join a religious order;
we are no longer children.
Everybody is an adult.
The religious orders hope to
treat their members
as grown-up people.
And the brothers and sisters
need to take time
to respond to each other
with care.
Listening is more than hearing.
Too many times
we hear something
and run around in circles
like Samuel
when he first heard God's voice.

Instead, stop!
"Listen, then, if you have ears!" (Mark 4:23)
says Jesus.
We have to stand
still
and ask God,
ask each other
to speak
and promise
to listen with open hearts.

Just as we learn to listen
as brothers and sisters,
religious orders have a big chance
to help the church
learn to listen
to what the Spirit is saying to the Church
through all her faithful people.

A community of listening adults means:
a community of respect,
a community of responsibility,
a community that is different from the world,
ready to serve people nearby and far away.

Some things to think about and talk about

What did you learn about obedience
when you were growing up?

What happened when you, or other people,
did not obey the leaders
of family, community or church?

Find somebody to talk to
about these experiences of obedience as you were growing up.
Talk one at a time.
Listen to the other person 100%,
and when it is your turn;
talk as honestly as you can.

Part 2:
Obedience Means Listening to the Bible

To be obedient, we listen to God:
we listen to God in the Bible.

As Anglicans we test our thoughts and decisions
with the Bible,
church teachings,
and by talking together.
We say
"Scripture, Tradition, and Reason."
Many people add

"Experience,"
just to be sure
everybody's voice gets heard.
It's not "Bible only,"
because some Bible teachings
do not fit the world today.
Like slavery.
Everywhere in the Bible it talks about slaves,
as if everybody has them.
But no Christian church today
teaches it is right
to have slaves.

The Bible helps us remember
we belong to God.
It challenges us,
with stories and teachings
from prophets and many other people.
Inspired by God,
in other times and places,
they figured out
what God wanted them to do.

In Isaiah we read a powerful story
about peace and justice:
"Wolves and sheep
will live together in peace,
and leopards will lie down
with young goats.
Calves and lion cubs
will feed together,
and little children
will take care of them.
Cows and bears
will eat together,
and their calves and cubs
will lie down in peace.
Lions will eat straw as cattle do.
Even a baby

will not be harmed
if it plays near a poisonous snake.
On Zion,
God's holy hill,
there will be nothing
harmful or evil.
The land will be full
of knowledge of the Lord
as the seas
are full of water." (Isaiah 11:6-9)
Isaiah saw God's vision
and told stories about what he saw.
These are hopes for a world
where there is no violence,
no danger.
They are meant
to make us think about our world
of violence and danger
and how God wants
to use us
to bring peace and justice.

The teachings of Jesus
are clear
in this Bible tradition.
He teaches about living differently
in a violent world,
and keeping to ways of living
that help people to be
free and respected.

Let's put
what the world says
side by side
with what the Bible says.
Sometimes we hear
a friend,
or we read in the newspaper,
"War is necessary."

"The earth is ours to do what we want with it."
"Women are less important than men."

But the Bible says:
"Happy are those who work for peace." (Matthew 5:9)
"The earth and everything in it belong to the Lord."
(1 Corinthians 10:26)
"So God created human beings, making them to be like himself.
He created them male and female..." (Genesis 1:27)

The Bible teaches us,
our Anglican tradition teaches us,
and our heart teaches us,
that God wants justice.

Listening to the Bible is prayer.
Prayer is the rock religious life is built on.
That is why we take time
every day at different times all day long
to pray.
In every service,
we read the Bible.
We listen to its message;
we think about people we care about.
The Bible can make us
think about problems
in our life and in the world.
It teaches us to ask God to help us,
to show us how to make a difference
for these people and situations.
We are the hands of Jesus in the world today.
We are the feet of Jesus in the world today.
As Saint Mary the Virgin shows us,
it is through listening
that we become pregnant
with God's Word and message.
By listening to the Bible
we learn how to give birth
to new life.

Some things to think about and talk about

Reading the Bible to make our faith stronger
is a very important part of religious life.
It is called *Lectio divina*.
Think about finding time every day
to read the Bible by yourself.

Have you ever felt a part of the Bible was written "just for you"?

Is there a Bible verse that calls to you
to change your life or join an order?

What part is that, and why does it feel so special to you?

Part 3:
Obedience Means Listening to our Founders

When we join an Order,
the first people
we all need to listen to
very carefully
are our founders.
These are the women and men
who started our communities
and wrote the Rules.
Finding out what is expected of us
is always the best place to start.

The challenge is to listen
in our hearts
to the Rule.
This might be hard because
it was written long ago
at a certain time in history,
by a particular person.

Knowing about those times
helps us understand
the best way to live out
the gift of our Order's Rule.
If we keep it as just a check-list to follow
we miss the point and the world seems small:
"Prayer: 6:00 a.m.
Silence: 12:00 p.m.
Dinner: 6:30 p.m.
Ask permission to go out. . ."
The list goes on, the heart is not moved.
In most cases,
these rules
big and small,
are supposed to help us
listen to God,
listen to each other,
and help us change our lives and
to be free.

When we don't listen carefully
the rules may not make us feel free.
Or maybe we see older brothers or sisters
not following them.
So we start looking for ways
to get around the rules.
When we look
for permission in the actions of others
to do something wrong,
we will almost always find it.

Being obedient
to our Founder's wisdom and teaching
starts with the invitation
to stop comparing ourselves to others
and start doing the right things
because we want to
do right.
Even when nobody is looking.

As beginners
our job is to let go of old ways of thinking
and to learn new ways.
Think of the rules
as one half of a conversation.
The community speaks,
we listen and respond,
and grow.

As we grow into community life,
we can see better
how much of our struggle
is self will.

The community's Founders
invite us:
to live with silence—
and listen better.
To check out our plans with each other—
and share our lives more fully and fix problems.
To be regular in prayer services—
and become people who pray
at all times.

Some communities
don't always give good reasons
for their rules.
They seem unreasonable
to a modern mind.
But the more I learned
why
we did or didn't do certain things,
the happier I was to accept
the rules
and to search out how to
live them in modern times.

Most of our founders
were deeply involved

in important issues of their day.
Our Constitutions, Statutes, Principles,
Rule of Life,
have reminders of these struggles.
The more we know about this history
the better we can learn how
to fulfill the visions of our Founders,
and why we have the rules that we have.

Knowing where we come from,
and why we do what we do
points us on the way forward.
The teachings of our Founders
can help us make choices
about our life and ministry
and help us be faithful and listen carefully
to the Spirit's call right now.

Some things to think about and talk about

Not all religious orders are the same.
If you are thinking about joining an order,
find out as much as you can about the founders
as well as modern-day members.

Who were the founders of your community?

What were some of the reasons they started your order?

What are some of the rules or ideas that go back to those early days?

How has your community changed over the years?

Part 4:
Obedience Means Listening to Each Other, Leaders and Members

We listen to God in the decisions of the community.
When we talk together,
with prayer and care,
at community meetings and other times,
we believe we are listening to the Holy Spirit.
Sometimes we stop
talking and listening
because people are angry.
Sometimes we are angry
or afraid,
or feel like we don't count.
Or talking stops
because leaders shut it down
and make members
do what they are told.
Mostly
this only makes matters
worse.

When brothers and sisters
are not listening
to each other,
often the first place
we hear problems in community life
is in the chapel.
In my house,
the early warning system
is when I hear brothers reading the psalms
each at his own speed.
I wonder why we cannot
listen to each other.

The other place
in community life

where problems show up,
when communication breaks down
and we stop listening to each other,
is in the use of money.
If a brother or sister
(especially one in charge)
does not use money fairly,
so everybody knows
how much there is,
who is getting it,
and why,
there will be problems.
Many community money problems
are problems
with telling the truth.

Telling the truth to each other
is a big part of being obedient.

We must talk about these trouble spots.
Sometimes we agree,
sometimes we don't agree.
When we think differently from
our leaders or the community
it is our holy duty to say so—
before decisions are made—
with love,
with respect,
with confidence.

The vow of obedience
teaches us to listen to God
and each other
because sometimes
our ideas are just
big-headed
self-important
thinking.

Obedience works best
when we are humble.

The leaders must listen
to the members.
The members must listen
to the leaders.

The hardest job for the leaders
is to be sure every voice is heard:
the oldest member,
the newest member,
the ones who love to talk a lot,
the ones who do not like to talk in groups.

Every new member brings a gift to the community.
The community must listen
to the new brother or sister
as much as they want the new person
to listen to the senior sisters and brothers.
Otherwise,
the community will die.

We learn to listen.
Some find it easy,
some find it very hard.
It is a skill we learn for community life.
And we can take courses
to get better listening skills.

We learn to take time with each other
to listen as obedient people.
When we say or think
"Hurry up!"
"Who is next?"
we are not listening to what people are saying.
Nor does talking in a pushy, bossy way
open up God's words
held in a shy person's heart and mind.

And if the shy person says
"I think just the same
as she or he just said,"
they are not giving God a chance
to make the truth fully known.
They are running away
from God's invitation
to tell the truth,
the truth which
God has given them.
God does not give
the whole answer
to every problem
to one person.
Part of the answer is given to one person,
part to another,
part to another.
When we start to talk with each other,
we begin to find out the whole answer.
We begin to see a new way forward.

Sometimes we save up
things to talk about.
Our brains become full
of our own thoughts
and we sit and wait
until we get our chance to speak,
not listening to those around us.
I have been told:
"You are not listening to me."
Then there is anger and hurt.
It may mean we just don't agree,
but it may also mean
I am not trying hard enough
to hear what others are saying.

Around the world
I meet with brothers.
Sometimes it is hard
to do the work we have to do

because we feel
shame,
anger,
fear.
We fear we are not good enough.
Nobody wants to talk
because they have heavy hearts.

So, a leader's job is
to help brothers and sisters grow.
Healing begins when
we invite the brothers or sisters to talk,
and to listen,
to let go of their heavy load.
We ask each other to tell the truth:
What do you feel bad about?
What are you angry about?
Tell it out!
And everybody must promise
to listen
and to stay in the room,
even if their feelings get hurt.
Because everybody will have a chance to speak.
Like the Bible says:
"The truth will set you free." (John 8:32)
Then we can see and hear
where God is speaking to us.
Then we can open ourselves
to God's healing power.
When one of us talks about feeling
shame,
fear,
guilt,
anger,
people listening with love
can give back
respect,
hope,
encouragement.

When the Chapter or Council
agrees to a plan
about anything,
everybody must follow the plan,
like it or not.
Not to follow a plan
decided by the group,
after everyone has had their say,
is wrong.
Not getting our way
all the time
is part of real life.
It is how God teaches us
we are not boss of the world.
Other people
may know better
than we do.
So we do it,
without grumbling.
And next year
we can talk about it
again.

People who listen carefully
are doing God's work.
Listening and speaking
and being heard
are the blessings of obedience
and the cement of community life.
This is why obedience is the first promise we make.

Some things to think about and talk about

Do you find it hard or easy to talk in large groups?
Can you say why?

Living in community,
much of our time is in meetings.

Most important decisions happen in meetings.
What are the main things you think are important
so everybody can share in a meeting?

What are some things the leader of the meeting can do
to help everybody feel comfortable talking?

Have you ever found yourself thinking
something different from the leaders of your community?

What did you do or say about it?

What happened?

Part 5:
Obedience Means Listening to our Inner Voice

The Anglican way
teaches
that everyone has a voice inside.
Our conscience,
that says, "This is right,"
or "This is wrong."
Nobody
can make us do something
that the inner voice tells us is evil.

But it is hard
to listen to our inner voice
by ourselves.
Our inner voice and thoughts
must be heard out loud.
We need to find a special person
we can talk to
who will not tell
anybody else.

We each need a spiritual director
who will listen
and then tell us
what they hear.
And ask the question:
"Where is God in all this?"
Sometimes the stories we tell
leave out
important things.
A good,
loving
spiritual director
can ask questions to help us
listen to ourselves
and listen to God.

We can really get into trouble
when we don't test our inner voice.
For example,
trouble comes when we fall in love
(we do, you know)
if we don't tell
our spiritual director.
We might listen only to ourselves,
and decide sex is okay,
because we are in love.

Every community has a responsibility
to figure out
how to help
every sister and brother
have a spiritual director.

Our inner voice
can also tell us
very hard,
very important
things to do
for justice and truth.

A famous story
is told about a German pastor,
Dietrich Bonhoeffer.
The story takes place during
World War Two.

Bonhoeffer knew Hitler's program
to kill the Jews and take over the world
was evil.
All ways to stop Hitler failed;
talking,
praying,
demonstrations,
letter writing:
nothing worked.
It even looked like
Hitler might win the war.

Bonhoeffer met with his friends.
They prayed.
And prayed.
And read their Bibles.
They talked together.

As he saw what was happening
in the world around him,
he understood
he might have to
do something wrong
to do the right thing.

To stop Hitler,
to stop the war,
to stop the planned killing
of over 6,000,000 people,
to stop the Nazi war
on the rest of Europe,
Bonhoeffer understood
Hitler must be killed.
And he decided to help.

That is a hard decision
when you follow Jesus Christ.
The Prince of Peace said
"Put your sword back in its place!" (John. 18:11)
Jesus died
on the cross
without a struggle,
without a fight.

Bonhoeffer
was a Christian pastor
and teacher.
Finally, he accepted
that he must act
with compassion for the world;
he must act
because he was a Christian.

He tried to kill Hitler,
and he failed.
Hitler had him killed
April 8, 1945.

The morning he was killed,
Bonhoeffer preached
to his fellow prisoners on this
Bible passage:
"Let us give thanks
to the God and Father of our Lord Jesus Christ!
Because of his great mercy
he gave us new life
by raising Jesus Christ
from death.
This fills us with a living hope." (1 Peter 1:3) [11]

The Nazi German soldiers
who ran the death camps
and shot Dietrich Bonhoeffer
said:

"We were only obeying our leaders.
We did nothing wrong." [12]

Some things to think about and talk about

Read Romans 13:1. What do you think about this?

Do you know of other people
who stood up
for the right thing
at a big cost to themselves?

Do you have a Spiritual Director
or trusted listener
to discuss important decisions with?

How can you help your community
get advisors
for brothers and sisters?

Part 6:
Obedience Means Listening to Nature

Listening to God
also means listening to and studying
the natural world.
As St. Paul says:
"Ever since God created the world,
his invisible qualities,
both his eternal power and his divine nature,
have been clearly seen;
they are perceived in the things
God has made." (Romans 1:20)

We get to know God better
by studying nature.
Knowing more about nature
helps us to to serve God
and take care of creation
as obedient people.

St. Francis
called sun, moon, stars
earth, winds and water
his brothers and sisters.
By listening to God (and science)
we discover
we are related
to every part
of nature.
What we do
makes a difference
to other creatures.
God said at Creation,
"I am putting you in charge," (Genesis 1:28)
so everything will come up for good.
But we spoiled nature
with too much smoke
in the air,
too many chemicals
in the ground and water.

When humans hurt nature,
crops fail,
water dries up,
people get sick,
people and fish and animals die.
Some people ask then,
"How does God want us to live?"

Comparing the creation story in the Bible
with the world today,
we know we have to

do something quick
or it will be too late.

Out of love for God
and his creation,
religious brothers and sisters
can show people
how to take care of the earth,
by listening to every creature.
Learn their secret ways.
Help all living beings to live
happy lives.
People must stop spoiling nature.
We can show people
how to use less chemicals,
to eat food from the garden,
how to live simple lives.

Human beings are part of nature, too.
It is important
that we listen to our bodies.
Our bodies are good.
God chose to have a body
when Jesus was born.
Our bodies can teach us how to live
the way God wants us to live.
When we feel tired,
or sick,
or angry,
or happy,
or sexy,
our bodies know it.
Our bodies never lie.

But many human beings
don't listen to their body.
We ignore feelings of hunger
or anger,
or loneliness,

or tiredness.
And we start to break down.
Then we do or say things
that hurt ourselves and other people.
We start telling lies:
"I am fine," we say,
when we should be in bed
drinking medicine.
"I am fine," we say
when we really need to say
our feelings are hurt.
We may say,
"I am okay"
because we don't want
to slow things down
or get in the way
or spoil anybody's plans.
So we learn to lie
about how we are feeling.
Then we get in trouble.
We spread germs,
we fight,
we stop listening or caring
and we spoil the group.

Listen to your body.
God has filled it with wisdom.

Now, I want to say a special word
about exercising obediently.
It is part of listening to our bodies.
To work right,
the way God wants,
we have to move our bodies,
get air into our lungs,
make the blood
pump.
Exercise is very important.
I have told some people

who come to me for spiritual direction,
"Try to sweat
two or three times a week,
at least."
Sometimes we sweat
working in the kitchen,
working in the garden,
sweeping the floors.
But it is good to go for a run,
or just walk fast,
or kick a ball,
or lift weights,
or swing our arms around,
or skip rope,
or swim,
or dance:
laugh, sweat, feel the sun and the rain,
feel alive.
Exercise takes away bad feelings.
It makes our bodies healthy;
it makes our minds clear
and it is easier to pray and think.

When I was forty-five
I started to run.
I ran because my body
felt weak.
I had pain in my back,
and I felt a little bit angry
all the time.
In other words,
I felt stress
in body, mind, and spirit.
I started slowly,
running a little at a time,
but soon I could go far.
We can feel God's love
in our bodies
when we exercise.

Feeling God's love
is what obedient living is all about.

Some things to think about and talk about

Draw a picture of a favorite place
you like to visit in nature.
Tell somebody why it is special to you.

Make a list of all the things you do in a week.

How much time do you have for sport
or exercise that is fun?

If you think you have no time,
for one day write down everything you do,
starting with chapel, prayer time, work
and cleaning.
Then add
how much time you spend on the computer,
or sitting around talking,
or sleeping during the day.

When I did this I learned
I will always have time to do the things
I really want to do.

To Sum Up: Important Teachings to Remember from this Chapter

1. Learning to listen
   is the foundation of obedience.

2. Listening to God in the Bible,
   we give new life to the world.
3. Listening to our founders we learn how to
   be faithful to the special gift of our community.
4. Listening to God in community
   we take responsibility for our religious life.
5. Listening to our inner voice
   we live for God against all evil;
   and everybody needs a trusted listener.
6. Listening to God in nature
   we take care of the natural world and our bodies,
   giving glory to God.

Our vow of obedience
is about shaping our lives
in connection with God:
"to serve God is perfect freedom"
as we pray in the Book of Common Prayer. [13]

Chapter 3: Poverty

Poverty can be confusing
because it is both a sin and a virtue,
both bad and good.
To be spiritually poor,
with nothing to give,
no relationship with God,
is bad.
To be poor in spirit,
humble,
dependent on God,
is good.
When people have nothing to eat
and no place to live,
it is wrong.
When religious brothers and sisters
choose to live together,
it is good.

I want to talk about four parts
of our vow of poverty.

Part 1: Religious poverty means following the example of Jesus.
Part 2: Religious poverty is freely chosen.
Part 3: Religious poverty helps us help the poor.
Part 4: Religious poverty makes our social vision clear.

Part 1:
Poverty Means Following the Example of Jesus

Here is a Scripture passage
about following the example
of the poverty of Jesus Christ:

"The attitude you should have is the one
that Christ Jesus had:
He always had the nature of God,
but he did not think
that by force
he should try to remain equal with God.
Instead of this,
of his own free will
he gave up all he had,
and took the nature of a servant.
He became like a human being
and appeared in human likeness.
He was humble and walked the path of obedience
all the way to death—
his death on the cross.
For this reason
God raised him to the highest place above
and gave him the name that is greater
than any other name.
And so, in honor of the name of Jesus
all beings in heaven,
on earth,
and in the world below
will fall on their knees,
and all will openly proclaim
that Jesus Christ is Lord,
to the glory of God the Father." (Philippians 2:5-11)

Over the years,
the example of Jesus
who "gave up all he had"
made many people
want to do the same thing.
Plus, Jesus says:
Go, "sell all you have
and give the money to the poor,
and you will have riches in heaven;
then come and follow me." (Luke 18:22)

Our vow of poverty
can bring us
very close to Jesus
if we live it honestly.
But it is not just about
living without money.

After living as a novice for a few years,
I was professed.
I took my vows of obedience, poverty and chastity.
It was a very happy day.
Many friends came to Little Portion Friary in New York, USA.
After the service
there was a feast of good food.

My friends wanted to know
about poverty.
"Look," they said,
pointing at the beautiful friary,
the big gardens:
"This is not like the way poor people live.
This looks like a house for rich people!"

"How do you explain this?" they asked.

I had a hard time trying to explain it.
But I said,
the brothers who came before me
built it,
loved it,
made it shine with beauty.

I cannot say their love was wrong.

I cannot do everything over,
just to make myself happy.
I cannot choose
how I want my brothers and sisters to be.
We are all beggars. [14]

Living with the decisions and actions of others
in community
is part of our vow of poverty.

This is also true
when people hurt us
in community.
Sometimes we are sad or mad,
but there is no way to "get even."
It is not God's way.
Jesus died on a cross.
And it cannot be the way
of religious orders.
Not getting even
when we feel hurt
is a kind of poverty.

My first lesson in religious poverty
was to understand,
even with my education
and ordination,
I am not the boss of the world.
I must think about who is:
God is in charge of the world.

Not even Jesus
tried to remain equal with God!
And that is the reason
St. Francis of Assisi decided to be poor. [15]
More than anything else,
Francis wanted to be like Jesus.
Francis knew how,
of his own free will,
Jesus gave up all he had
and lived like a servant.
So, of his own free will,
Francis gave up all he had
to serve people and God.
He did it because Jesus did it. [16]

St. Clare wanted to be like Jesus, too [17]
following the example of St. Francis.

Both of them gave away
all their money and clothes
and all the power
of being children of rich people.
They no longer had power to boss people,
because they had no money
to pay them or not pay them.
They soon realized they had
to give up
their own will, wanting things done their way;
to give up
being important people in charge of things;
to give up
taking money because people wanted to pay
for their teaching and sermons;
to give up
being angry about what other people do;
to give up
feeling special,
because they gave these things up. [18]

Francis and Clare
are only two of many people
who have lived the life we are living as vowed religious.
Their experience is important,
even if you are not a Franciscan.
Their experience makes us think about
what we mean
when we talk of poverty,
why you do it,
how you do it.
Francis and Clare did not become poor
to count things,
or to shame a rich church,
or because a wise person
told them to be poor,

or even to make their life
more productive.
They became poor because Jesus was poor.

If we forget Jesus,
poverty makes us unhappy.
Nobody likes giving up things
for no reason at all.
Human beings always want more, more, more!

Without Jesus we count
how many books a brother has,
how often sister eats in a restaurant,
we check
who has a cell phone.
We get angry and argue
about should we have a car
or a computer
or take a course.
We say these things are against poverty.

What would Jesus say?
What would Francis say?

I think he would say,
counting things
is small-minded. [19]
It is a way to look
over a brother's or sister's shoulder:
"Just checking," we say,
"to see if you are poor enough."
Maybe what we really mean is:
"Just checking to see
that you do not have more than me."
Instead of saying
"poverty, poverty,"
we need to start
talking about what we need
for healthy life and work.

For many of us,
no money is a real problem.
We have to depend on God's help
to survive.
Many times for religious orders
on the edge of total poverty,
a gift comes.
Some good people
help religious orders.
God makes it possible
through them
for many of us to live.
This has been the case
since Joanna, Susanna and Mary Magdalene
paid the bills
for Jesus and his followers. (Luke 8:3)
Even when we don't choose poverty,
we can choose
how we live with it.
Over and over
the Bible tells us
"Trust in the Lord."
"The Lord will provide."
Francis calls it
"going to the table of the Lord"
when we ask for help from others.
Poverty is a way to show how much faith we have.

Because we want
to follow the example of Jesus,
our vow of poverty
makes sense.
No matter if we start out
as poor people before religious lives
or if we start out as rich people,
Jesus' way
of being poor
is to put our life
in God's hands.

When we do this,
a vow of poverty
brings joy.

Some things to think about and talk about

Talk with somebody about what the example of Jesus
means to you in your vow of poverty.

Take some time to read and to pray this prayer about giving up
everything for Jesus.
It is by St. Ignatius of Loyola,
a Roman Catholic saint who lived
in the 16th century in Spain.
He founded a religious order called
The Society of Jesus.

Take, Lord, and receive all my liberty,
my memory, my understanding
and my entire will,
all I have and call my own.
You have given all to me.
To you, Lord, I return it.

Everything is yours; do with it what you will.
Give me only your love and your grace.
That is enough for me. [20]

Part 2:
Religious Poverty is Freely Chosen

Let's take another look
at the poverty of Jesus.
When we read the Bible
we see Jesus
had food to eat,
friends to share it with.
He was a guest
in people's houses.
He had clothes to wear,
clothes so nice
the soldiers drew straws
to get them
after nailing him to the cross.
Jesus' poverty
was not to be equal with God,
to be humble and poor in spirit,
and to trust in God.

So, we cannot say
the vow of poverty means we have to go
hungry,
homeless,
or naked.
A few brothers or sisters may have a special call
to live this way.
Such a special call is a real blessing.
But many others find it too hard to do.

But when we meet people
hungry,
homeless,
naked,
they are suffering,
and it is wrong.

In religious life
we *decide* to be poor:
to give away
our money,
to move out
of our house into one
we share with other people.
We choose
to have the same things
as everybody else
in the community.
In some communities
we choose
to give up other things,
like alcohol, that can spoil
religious life
when we drink too much.
We turn in our pay checks,
if we get one,
because we give up personal bank accounts, too.
We put our books
into the house library
when we are done with them.
If we leave the community
we cannot say
"I earned this,"
"This is mine."

I have discovered
that because we live together
our poverty
makes us depend on each other.
Our dependence makes our life bigger.
We have more time,
more freedom.

When everything is going right
everybody
in the religious order

works together
to take care of things
according to their ability.
We clean together,
cook together,
build and repair buildings together—
the list goes on.

When everybody works together
we get it done faster.
We are free
to live Spirit-led lives:
to pray,
to read,
to study,
to visit sick people
and people in prison,
to teach,
to live out our dreams
of serving others,
to share the Good News of Jesus.

When members of religious orders
choose to live together
we show society
where many people want more things,
where many people are trying to go faster,
save money,
and get power,
that it is possible
to choose simpler lives
with rich rewards.

Some things to think about and to talk about

What is the story you tell yourself about poverty?

If you are thinking about making religious vows
how do you feel about being poor like Jesus?

How important is poverty to your call
to be a brother or sister?

How does your community decide about
what poverty looks like for your community?

Part 3:
Religious Poverty Helps Us Help the Poor

There are many kinds of poverty.
Two kinds we work to change
are spiritual poverty
and economic poverty.

In the Bible,
there is a good kind of spiritual poverty
which means to be humble.
There is another kind that
causes trouble for people.
They think they know everything,
but they know
nothing about God,
nothing about peace in their life.
They are poor
from spiritually empty lives.
For example, they could be
tired, sick and poor
from drinking too much,
tired, sick and poor
from gambling.

We work to fight
spiritual poverty
with encouragement,
education;
lovingly telling the truth to people
when we see them sick and tired.

We help these poor
with our prayers,
with our friendship,
with liturgy
and spiritual counsel.

Economic poverty
makes people suffer.
They do not choose it.
It means not enough food.
It means being sick
and having no medicine or health care.
It means houses
that are not strong,
the rain coming through the roof,
the heat going out,
everything spoiled and the people
uncomfortable.
Sometimes it means
their education is not good enough
to get a job.
Sometimes it means
there are just no jobs to get.

We fight it by helping
where and how we can,
to show how real our love is,
by bringing rich and poor together,
by standing up for poor people
in front of lawmakers,
and reminding Christians
of their poor brothers and sisters in Christ.
St. Paul gives us a challenge:
"I am not laying down any rules.
But by showing
how eager others are to help,
I am trying to find out
how real your own love is."
(2 Corinthians 8:8)

Spiritually poor people
cause many of the problems
for the economically poor.
Economic poverty is made worse
by spiritual poverty:
corruption,
government pay-offs,
greed of the richest nations
are examples of spiritual poverty
making the economically poor
poorer.

Once in New York
we were a small group of brothers,
five of us.
Some were sick or old.
But we still felt called
to help the poor.
We decided
to give small grants
to people doing ministry
with poor people
from money we earned
working together
baking bread.
We put up a sign
saying
"If you want a grant
for your ministry,
send us a letter."
We got many letters.

And many rich people
(economically and spiritually rich)
saw the sign, too.
They gave us more money
so there was plenty
to go around.

Another time
my brothers in New York
decided
to help some workers
who had come to America
without visas,
because they were too poor
to pay the fees.
They came because
they were very hungry.
They saw America as a rich country
with many jobs.
And they had no place else to go.

They came to America
and worked hard.
But many people hated them,
saying they took jobs from Americans.
Only no Americans
wanted to do the jobs
they did:
cutting grass,
washing dishes in restaurants.
The workers needed
a place to meet.
They wanted to find ways
to support each other
and to make peace
with the Americans.

The local political leaders
said they would make
anybody who helped
the workers
pay more taxes
as a punishment.

The brothers prayed
about this threat.

We had no money
to pay taxes,
but we believed
we had to help the workers.
Other churches (not all)
said they could not help,
because they were afraid
of paying the taxes.

We opened our house,
so that the workers
could meet.
We expected twelve men;
400 came!
We became friends with them,
giving them a place to meet.
Every couple of months
they helped clean
our gardens
as a "thank you" to the brothers.
We cooked dinners for them,
and we all ate together.

We never
had to pay more taxes.
We fed them,
helped them,
and we keep on working
to change the laws,
even to this day.

Some things to think about and to talk about

What do you give away in order to help others?
How do challenge corrupt leaders?
How do you work to heal spiritual poverty?

Part 4:
Religious Poverty Makes our Social Vision Clear

When we
listen to,
eat with,
work with
poor people
we learn to see the world
differently.

With billions of people
going hungry,
the economically poor
teach us to ask:
why are some people rich
and so many people poor?
Why don't rich people
share their money
with the poor?
How do rich people
(and countries) stay rich?

If we ask ourselves
these questions,
we have to ask other people
these questions
to find out some answers.

People do not go hungry
because there is no food in the world.
But because they cannot get
the food.
Did you know
the earth produces enough food
to feed
every single human being?

Every single one,
nobody left out?
It does.
Right now. [21]

But the richest nations
use the most resources.
They use grain,
which could feed people,
to make fuel for cars
and to feed cows
to kill for meat.
This grain,
that could feed
over 1 billion people,
goes to America
and other rich nations
for cars and hamburgers. [22]

A question:
How long will this go on?
Who are you going to ask?

When you ask the right question
to the right person,
then people,
communities,
countries
change.

England changed
about slavery.
It happened because William Wilberforce
started asking, was it right?
He kept asking
and got others to ask
Parliament.
England abolished slavery in 1833. [23]

South Africa changed
about the evil system of
keeping black people
separate from whites
and keeping them poor and without rights.
It happened because Nelson Mandela
and the Anglican Archbishop of Capetown,
Desmond Tutu, and many others
started asking, is it right?
They taught the world
to boycott South Africa.
They asked: How can the civilized world
allow this to go on? [24]

Burma is changing
from a dictatorship
into a democracy.
Because Aung San Suu Kyi
for over twenty years
spoke up for the poor people of Burma,
even when she was under house arrest.
Now she is in parliament
helping to change her country. [25]

Change comes
when men and women
take the side of the poor
and start asking questions,
showing up lies
and corruption.

If you can't think
of any questions,
read the United Nations
Universal Declaration of Human Rights.
(See the back of this book.)

Jesus wanted
justice

for the world.
He became poor
to serve God,
to serve the world,
to give honor
to God.

Our vow of poverty
is to be like Jesus,
to be like the poor in the questions we ask
to be with the poor,
to be with Jesus.

The vow of poverty
is a call
to conversion,
to give our lives,
to help all who suffer
and are poor
in body, mind and spirit.
It is a call
to leave our comfort zone
and enter
the Kingdom zone.

Some things to think about and talk about

When poor people come to see you,
or you visit the poor,
the sick,
the people you know in prison,
what are the questions
that keep you awake at night?

Who can you ask for answers
to your questions?

To Sum Up: Important Teachings to Remember from this Chapter

1. We follow the example of Jesus' poverty
   by remembering God is in charge,
   and putting our life in God's care.
2. By choosing religious poverty,
   we depend on our brothers and sisters.
3. Religious men and women fight both
   spiritual and economic poverty.
4. Seeing the world from the point of view of the poor
   we can ask questions
   and change social conditions.

Chapter 4: Chastity

For lots of people
chastity is a deal breaker.
Many think it is the opposite
of Good News!

I want to talk about four different parts of the vow of chastity:

Part 1: What do we mean by chastity and celibacy?
Part 2: What are good reasons for taking this vow?
Part 3: What about sexy thoughts and feelings?
Part 4: How does chastity help tell out the Good News
 of Jesus Christ?

This Bible passage teaches
"purity of heart" is what chastity is about:
Jesus said: "Happy are the pure in heart; they will see God."
(Matthew 5:8) [26]

Part 1:
What Do We Mean by Chastity and Celibacy?

First of all,
chastity is not just about sex.
Chastity teaches us
to pray for pure hearts,
not to say mean words,
not to laugh when others hurt,
not to fight,
not to tell stories against people. [27]
Because chastity
means shaping our lives
around the gifts of the Spirit:
"love,

joy,
peace,
patience,
kindness,
goodness,
faithfulness,
humility,
and self-control." (Galatians 5:22)
It is about truth and faithfulness
with gentleness,
in all things.

My first lesson in chastity
happened after dinner
soon after I joined
the brothers.
I said, "That was terrible food."
I spoke too loudly and
the brother who cooked
felt very hurt
and angry.
"How would you like somebody
to say that to you?"

Chastity
also means
no grudges:
don't hate your brothers or sisters.
Don't say,
every time there is a problem,
"Brother so-and-so must have done it."

I am very careful,
when I stand up for social justice,
not to let hatred and anger
be in my every word and action.
Chastity is about wholeness and balance.

Chastity
is also when we are happy about our feelings about sex,
happy with the people we love,
happy with our bodies,
happy with the choices we make
as baptized Christians
about all our life,
how it all fits together
—with no lying or trouble for ourselves
or others.

For members of some religious communities,
it is possible to make a promise of chastity
and be married
and enjoy sex.
For instance,
members of the Third Order of the Society of St. Francis do this. [28]
If you are married,
chastity means
no sex outside marriage,
to be faithful to your husband or wife.
If you are not married
chastity means no sex,
because Anglicans teach
sex and marriage go together.

Celibacy is a little different
from chastity,
but they go together in many religious orders.
For brothers and sisters
it means you choose
not to marry,
to serve the Kingdom of God.

Celibacy
can be a stumbling block.
Because no sex
is very personal.
Many of us struggle with it,

and there is no way
not to struggle.
It can feel like a big burden.
The joy comes from learning
everyday
who I am,
what I really want from life.
Adults are responsible
and choose one thing over another.

Not everybody thinks celibacy is such a good thing.
Some people say
celibacy is bad.
Look at the troubles
in the Roman Catholic Church
with some priests having sex
with young people.

Some people say:
"Do away with celibacy,
let priests marry.
The sex abuse problems will go away!"
The problem is not so simple.
There are many other things
that go into this problem:
for example,
some priests feel
they have nobody to talk to
about sex feelings,
or loneliness.
Poor training,
and church leaders keeping secrets
add to the problem, too.
All of these
are more to blame than
celibacy itself.

Some sex abusers
are married people.

Celibacy does not make you more likely
to hurt people.
But because of celibacy
many men
stay away from ordained ministry
in the Catholic Church.
They do not like
being *forced* to be celibate
in order to serve
in the Church.

Anglicans have never said
you had to be celibate
to be a minister.
But if you feel called to live this way,
for a few years
or for your whole life,
Anglicans have made room
for God's calling.
It is the job of the religious orders
to help
sisters and brothers
figure out
if they are called by God
to live celibate lives.
Otherwise, it can cause
spiritual harm.

Sometimes brothers and sisters say,
because they are not married,
they are single.
Not true.
Our vows are as important as wedding vows.
Only different.
We are not free
like a person with no vows
to have special sex relationships.

But not getting married
and not having sex

does not mean
having no friends.
Friendship with all kinds of people
was very important for Jesus.
He made friends with
"outcasts and sinners."
Do you?
It was how he shared his message.

Having friends both inside and outside
the community
helps us to give and receive love.
It also helps us learn
how to tell the truth about our life
and our commitments
to other people.
To live the vow of chastity
as celibates,
we need friends who know and love us
as brothers and sisters,
who can listen and encourage us
to be faithful to our vows.
We need friends who can laugh with us,
when times are tough.
Friends can make us feel
somebody cares
when the cares of life
are too much.

When we talk
about our vow of chastity
and celibacy
we are talking about
the gift of God,
to love and be loved,
and to keep on loving
in a very special way.

Some things to think about and to talk about

What does chastity mean to you?

Can you say why
not getting married
might be God's call to you?

Can you describe somebody who has taken a vow of chastity
and what you like most about them?

If you don't know any religious,
what are your hopes and fears
about chastity and celibacy?

What does chastity have to do
with things you feel very strongly about,
like talk about money?
Or church politics?

Part 2:
What Are Some Good Reasons for Taking the Vow of Chastity?

People only think about
taking a vow of chastity and celibacy
because deep down they believe
this is how God
wants them to live.

By doing what God wants,
we believe
we will be happy and peaceful
in our life.
So, a first good reason
to take a vow of chastity
and be celibate

is to be happy and faithful
to God's call.

Second, there are reasons from the Bible
to be celibate.
Jesus said,
"[some] do not marry
for the sake of the kingdom of Heaven." (Matthew 19:12)
and St. Paul said,
"Actually I would prefer
 that all of you were as I am..."
[that is, not married] (1 Corinthians 7:7-8)
This is why
some Christians have had the idea
not to marry
and to live in religious orders.
Our example
can encourage all Christians
to think how to give their lives
to God
body, mind and spirit,
according to God's call.

A third good reason to take this vow
is to enjoy freedom
to serve God without worry.
Again, St. Paul tells the Corinthians:
"I would rather spare you the everyday troubles
that married people have." (1 Corinthians 7:28)
People with children
worry about caring for them,
paying school fees,
doctor's bills,
and other things
parents need to pay for.
If you are married and have children,
you cannot risk their life
and be a good parent.
Little children are not free

to agree to no health care,
poor education,
no clothes!
But if you have no wife
or husband
or family,
you can go on mission,
risk your health to help others,
live in places
that may not be good places
to raise a family,
but wonderful places
to serve God.

Another good reason
to take a vow of chastity
is all your energy
can go to God.
We can get up early
and stay up late to pray,
to be alone with God in prayer.

For many of these good reasons,
it is possible to say
"Yes, but..."
because married people
can do these things too.
Married people also serve God.
They also can live chaste and faithful lives.
There is no contest
between Religious and married people.

The choice not to marry is not better
than the decision to marry.
St. Paul only said "I prefer," not "I require."
It all depends on God's call to you.

Religious brothers and sisters
get no special credit

because we take a vow of chastity or celibacy,
any more than married people
get special credit for their vows.
If brothers and sisters
do not use their vow
to live BIG lives,
taking risks,
they are wasting a big chance
to experience
the special joy
of religious life.
Choosing to live in community,
choosing to live without sex,
is a loving, trusting response to God
who can help us
give our life to others.
Our love has to go somewhere,
so we pour it out
with creativity and love
in our personal prayer time,
in taking part in church services,
and in serving Christ
in every person we meet.

Things to think about and talk about

Mahatma Gandhi was a man
who helped India get free from Great Britain in 1948.
A man who wrote a story about Gandhi's life,
Jad Adams,
reported in an English newspaper,
Gandhi wanted "to give service
to humanity,
and decided it must
be by embracing
poverty
and chastity [sexual abstinence].
At age 38, in 1906

he took a vow of
brahmacharya,[a Hindu word]
which meant
living a spiritual life
but is normally referred to as
chastity [sexual abstinence]
without which such a life is thought
impossible by Hindus...
With the zeal
of a convert,
within a year of his vow
he told readers of his newspaper
Indian Opinion:
'It is the duty
of every thoughtful Indian
not to marry.
In case he is helpless
in regard to marriage,
he should abstain
from sexual intercourse with his wife.'" [29]

Gandhi did not mean
never having children.
But he found a way to make a
spiritual teaching
help him in his work to promote peace and non-violence.

What do you think about this?
Do you think
not having sex
can be a help to your spiritual life?
A help to serve your God or your country?

How might chastity and a celibate commitment
help you become
the best person you can be?

Part 3:
What about Sexy Thoughts and Feelings?

This section talks about something
I have been asked about
many, many times!
"Are sexy thoughts and feelings sinful?"
I don't believe they are sinful.

Sexy thoughts
will show up in our prayers:
strong feelings in our minds
and changes in our bodies
happen to us:
they are part of human life.
Sexy thoughts and feelings
teach me
to be honest with myself and God.
And to ask for God's help.
If I lie to myself or others
about my feelings,
it is like a storm inside me,
spoiling my prayer,
making me feel
a little bit crazy,
a little bit sad.
But when I am honest
I can pray
"Take me just as I am, Lord,
use me for your Kingdom.
With your love make me the man
you know me to be."

Every brother and sister
knows about
long nights of temptation.
We must choose
over and over again
to give ourselves

to God's call.
In time, with God's help,
we learn important
skills of chastity.
We learn
not to talk about sex
all the time,
not to read too many sexy books
not to look at sexy pictures.
We learn to think about other things.
After all, it is only possible
to think about one thing at a time,
so we keep coming back to God.

The spiritual trap
is all-or-nothing thinking.
We think falling in love or sexy feelings
prove that God doesn't want us to be
a brother or sister.
We think if we have a calling
we should not feel these things.
The truth about the feelings
is that they have no power
except what we give them.
I think
God wants us to enjoy the feelings—
it is like putting our hands
in a stream of water:
we can't control or catch it,
it just washes over us,
leaving us happy,
refreshed,
and the water keeps going
in the stream
and we keep going
in our life in community.
We keep praying,
trusting,
talking to our advisors.

As I said
at the beginning
of this book,
I joined
the religious order with
lots of questions about sex.
I found it confusing.
At last,
talking about these questions
with my spiritual director
I experienced
great healing.
My healing process
opened this part of my life
to God.
The more I understood myself
the easier it was
to see God active
in this part of my life.

My choice
to be celibate
grew stronger
as I learned
sex could not fix me;
only God could
if I trusted in his love,
and gave my life to him.

But even trusting in God,
life takes
interesting turns.
No matter
what we say
before we join,
after we join a religious order
many (not everybody)
are surprised
to fall in love,

at one time
or another.

Being in love is beautiful.
It is deeply connected
with being happy.
But for a religious
it can be
very disturbing
and make us feel
crazy.
For most of us,
just as a cyclone is
not the end of the world,
a storm of sexy or loving feelings
does not have to mean
the end of our vowed commitment.
Hot feelings grow cold.
Go slowly.
But if it happens to you,
you need the community
more, not less,
to figure it out.
Keep asking for help
from your spiritual director,
your brothers and sisters.

Are we ever called away
by God
from religious life
by falling in love with somebody?
Yes.
Things can change in life.
After praying a lot
and talking with a
spiritual director over time,
we can possibly say
God is calling us out
of religious life
to marriage or something else.

To leave,
especially after life vows,
is like a divorce.
But because some people leave
does not mean life vows
are impossible
or don't count.

We can love deeply,
freely,
without sex.
It takes prayer,
patience,
trust
and forgiveness—
our tap roots in the spiritual life.
Many religious are able
to use the experience
to become stronger in their commitment
to God
and their community,
and enjoy deep friendships.

God does not call us
only to drop us in times of trouble
and temptation
or to make us suffer.
God is with us,
showing us the way.
If God wants us
to be religious brothers and sisters,
God will answer our prayers
and help us
to find ways
to be happy
that fit our calling and life choice.

Things to think about and talk about

When sexy thoughts and feelings
show up in your prayer life,
practice letting them go.
Think about
putting the thoughts in a basket
and setting them aside.
Maybe think about placing them
at the foot of the Cross.

Or make them the subject of your prayer:
this means to pray
and ask God to help you
pray about the persons or feelings.

Sometimes I make a list
of all the things
that make my prayer life hard
as I am praying.
Writing down a word or sentence
gets the thoughts out of my mind.
Then I can go back
to my meditation.

Talk about other ways you have
to deal with things
that get in the way
of your praying.

Even when the prayer
has been a struggle
with sexy thoughts and feelings,
say "thank you" for God's grace and help.
Sometimes that is
the best we can do today.

Part 4:
How Does Chastity Help Us Tell Out the Good News of Jesus Christ?

Because chastity
means to live with love,
joy,
peace,
patience,
kindness,
goodness,
faithfulness,
humility,
and self-control,
this vow helps us
to give ourselves to God
and others
for the sake
of the Good News.

Chastity
is a level to aim for
in our spiritual life.
By giving ourselves
to God
we can find
humility,
peace of mind,
self-control
in God's time,
not on demand.

It counts
even if we feel
peace of mind
for only a few moments
in a day.

Just enough.
And it will get better.

This is an important point
when we talk about
our life with others:
"Yes, different as the religious life is,
hard as human life can be,
we experience
love,
joy and peace."
As we pray about it,
and ask for it,
and try to fit our lives to it
we are experiencing
a blessing of chastity.
People can see
what Christian conversion
and commitment is like
even if they
don't want to join
a religious order.

Being in a community
where everybody has taken
a vow of chastity,
I am helped
to live at peace
with others and
without fear,
with joy,
thankful to God.
Because I feel
loved and supported,
I feel able
to share honestly
with other people.
They encourage me
and I encourage them.

Along with this,
we learn
to love many people
with hands open,
not holding tight,
but giving others freedom.
To be loved freely,
not having to give back
or promise anything—
just loved and cared for—
is a great gift in anybody's life.
It is how God loves us.

Our vow of chastity can change human customs.
Living in single-sex communities
we have to do many things
differently from our culture.
In religious orders
everybody must work
for the community.
"Women's work" and "men's work"
are all mixed together.
St. Paul wrote to the Galatians
that, in Christ, there is no difference
"between men and women." (Galatians 3:28)
Not being married
is a challenge to brothers and sisters
to live in a new way,
to express
the gifts God gives them.
Sometimes it may not feel like a gift,
"This is women's work,"
some brothers say sometimes.
"We need a man to do this,"
a sister might think.
Then our minds change.
When our minds change,
the world changes.

The vow of chastity
helps us see through
the way the world shows people
as valuable
because they are sexy and beautiful,
or smart,
or successful and rich.
We give up thinking
judging thoughts about others.
As St. Paul says to all Christians:
"No longer, then,
do we judge anyone
by human standards...
When anyone is joined to Christ,
he is a new being;
the old is gone, the new has come." (2 Corinthians 5:16a, 17)
We see Jesus
in all people.

By loving people
because they are human beings
loved by God,
we can see their holiness.
Chastity helps us tell the Good News by:
1) calling us to give ourselves to others,
2) giving us times of inner peace,
3) encouraging us to love people freely,
4) making us live differently in our cultures,
5) helping us to see Christ in all people.

To see the world differently,
with God's eyes,
makes religious brothers and sisters
prophets.

We are prophets of love.
A love that frees us and other people
to be the people
God made us to be.

Some things to think about and talk about

How does chastity
help you find inner peace?

In what ways do you look at the world differently
because of your commitment
to chastity?

As you pray about chastity,
what is your hope for your life?

To Sum Up: Important Teachings to Remember from This Chapter.

1. Chastity means accepting the gifts of the Holy Spirit to live with love, joy, peace, patience, kindness, goodness, faithfulness, humility and self-control.
2. Celibacy means we are called by God not to marry and this gives us time for prayer and freedom for service.
3. Sexy thoughts and feelings are natural, and we learn not to let them rule our life.
4. Chastity and celibacy help us tell out the Good News by showing how people can live differently and by different standards.

Chapter 5:
Living the Vows and Prayer

St. Paul wrote to the Thessalonians:
Be joyful always
pray at all times,
be thankful
in all circumstances.
This is what
God wants from you
in your life in union with Christ Jesus.
(1 Thessalonians 5:16-18)

In this book
I have talked a lot
about prayer.
I want to say a few more words
about prayer,
especially
prayers of thanksgiving or gratitude.
Praying all the time
is the only way
to be truly happy
in religious life.

About prayer—
we pray as we can, not as we can't.
Some like to sit still
with eyes closed.
Others like to move around.
Some say special words
over and over to themselves.
Others keep their minds still.
Everybody can pray.
It is not just words we pray,
but when our hearts are open
to God.
We truly pray groans, sighs,

tears and laughter
and many more things like these.

Sometimes when we pray
with words or without
we ask God for help,
we ask God for forgiveness,
we ask God for food,
we ask God for love,
we ask God for everything.
And this is very good.

Sometimes when we pray,
we thank God for his help,
we thank God for happy endings,
we thank God for food,
we thank God for new jobs,
we thank God for every good thing in our lives.
And this is very good.

How does prayer work?
Who starts the prayer?
That is a good question!

God starts the prayer.
When we want to pray,
that feeling is a gift from the Holy Spirit.
Even when we say:
"God help me!"
why are we thinking of God?
Because God puts that thought
in our heads.

God starts the prayer,
we answer back:
"Our Father!" we say.
or
"Please help me..."
or

"Thank you..."
or
"Amen: so be it!"

Then,
we offer ourselves to God:
God uses us to touch lonely people,
God uses us to heal sick people,
God uses us to teach people,
God uses us to take care of the earth,
God uses us to stop violence and wars.
God uses us to make the world
a clean place,
a fair place,
a place of justice,
a place of peace,
a place of hope.

There are many different ways
of opening the door of our hearts
when God knocks:
in silence,
in singing,
in reading the Bible,
in going to church,
in making friends with people
we might feel nervous around.
In spending time
with people different from us,
in just looking
at people, places and things,
and letting our hearts
be touched:
all of these
are part of prayer,
being open to God.
The great joy
is that we never
finally
become experts on prayer.

As brothers and sisters
in religious orders
we spend our whole life
learning to open up
more and more to God,
the source of love,
peace,
wholeness.
Our communities
give us special times
to pray together,
out loud
and silently.
It is important
to use the times of silence
as times to be with Jesus in prayer.

Another chance to be with Jesus
is when we celebrate Holy Communion.
Being with Christ in the Sacrament
helps us
give our whole life
to him.

Thinking about our vows,
we ask for God's help.
We need to thank God
for this great chance
to live this way,
even when it feels
very hard
and we are sad and frustrated.

Some people thank God
when bad things happen
(I know this is hard to do).
Bad things are still bad,
no question.
But we don't want

to be a prisoner of bad times,
so we ask for God's help
to break out
into a new way of thinking.
Maybe you know the story in the Bible
of Joseph,
who was sold as a slave
by his brothers.
In the book Genesis,
after he has become Governor over Egypt,
Joseph tells his brothers:
"Now do not be upset
or blame yourselves
because you sold me here.
It was really God
who sent me ahead of you
to save people's lives." (Genesis 45:5)
Joseph is a powerful example to us
of how to find
the work of God
in hard situations,
and gives us the challenge
to do the same thing.
Instead of feeling sorry
for ourselves
or hating people
we think have done something to us,
we can ask,
"Can anything good,
or helpful
come out of this?"

What about if we said
"thank you" to God
for everything,
easy and hard,
in our religious life?

When I stopped drinking
I heard a man say:
"I thank God
I am an alcoholic."
I was shocked.
I would never say that!
I prayed hard
NOT TO BE an alcoholic,
I prayed hard
for God to take away my problem,
to make me clean.
I prayed hard
and said I was sorry
and would try to be better.
But to pray hard
and say "thank you"
for the worst thing
that ever happened to me?
NEVER!

Yet
as I have listened
over the years,
I learned that the people who say
"thank you"
for being alcoholic,
mean:
"Thank you for all the good things
that have happened
since I stopped drinking."
"Thank you
for all I have learned
about myself, good and bad."
"Thank you
for a new way of living
that depends on God."
"Thank you
for making me the way I am
so I can help other suffering people."

"Thank you
because if I were not alcoholic,
I would never learn these things."

So, I started to say
"thank you" to God.
I don't always remember,
but it makes a big difference.
When I forget to pray
or am too lazy to pray,
life gets harder:
I feel angry,
I feel alone.
When the pain
gets bad enough,
I hear God telling me
I need to do my part
to make my life better.
I need to open up to God,
to ask for God's help,
to thank God.

When we practice opening to God in prayer
God uses us
to say and do
the right thing
at the right time.
We become ready instruments
of his peace.

Some things to think about and talk about

Tell a story about how you pray.
Do you pray about your vows?

How do you pray when challenges happen?

Try writing a short list
of things you are grateful for,

every night before you go to bed.
It can change the way you see your life
and give God a chance
to show his love for you.

To Sum Up: Important Teachings to Remember from This Chapter

1. Prayer is the foundation of our vowed life.
2. Prayer is about being open to God
   and helping to make the world a better place.
3. Saying "thank you" to God for good and bad things
   can free us from the prison
   of anger and fear.

Chapter 6: Putting It All Together

The Vows and Creating the Kind of World We Want to Live in [30]

In this book
I have tried to show
how the vows
are something we can use
when we face
the challenges of life.
Out of the vows
we get skills
and ways of thinking
which can help us
as we work with the Holy Spirit
to be creative in ministry
and be healers
of the sick and suffering.

Because we make vows
to God
it is harder
to change our minds
about commitments
when life gets hard.

The vows protect
in us
deep down
the courage and strength
to live for God,
to help God
create a world
we want to live in,
a world of love.
Our world
is full

of violence,
poverty,
no education,
sickness,
pollution.
Either we can live
with all this,
or we can choose
to change it,
doing whatever we can
to shine the light of Christ
all around us.

In order to change
we need to make
the hard choice to love
at hard times—
times when we want to say,
"I hate you."
"I hurt too much."
"I don't know what to do."
"I am only one person."
"We need more money."
"It's not my problem."
All of these things
we might say
when we are hurting very much,
physically or spiritually.

The experience of God's love
in prayer
can help us
choose to be open to change
for ourselves.
And when we are changed by God's love,
we can help
other people
be open to God in prayer.
Together we can begin

the work
of creating
a world we want to live in.

I know a brother
in the Anglican
Society of the Sacred Mission,
Father Michael Lapsley,
who was sent by his Order
to work in South Africa.
He joined the fight
to end apartheid,
the South African government policy
that said
blacks and whites
must stay apart.
Completely separate.
And the white government
made sure
the blacks got the worst
of everything.
In his book,
Redeeming the Past:
My Journey from Freedom Fighter to Healer,
Father Lapsley writes:
"I was sent a letter bomb
that took away
my hands and one eye
but failed to kill me,
just as the brutality
of apartheid
failed
to crush the aspirations
of the South African people.
I returned to South Africa,
where I soon saw
that everyone
had been damaged
by the apartheid years

and had a story to tell,
and I resolved
to become a healer
of the nation." [31]

From there he became
a wounded healer
with a global mission.
Because millions of people
suffer all over the world
from violence,
Michael Lapsley
answered God's call
to make a difference
out of his terrible
situation.
He started
The Institute for Healing Memories.
Now he travels
to countries everywhere
listening to people,
serving them,
helping them to experience
real love,
real hope,
real peace.
And he invites them
to share this work. [32]
Healing and peace
spread
wherever he goes.

So, this story
is the hope of our calling:
to serve,
bringing new life and love
out of the grave
of damaged bodies,
out of our fear

and weakness.
It is to give thanks
for all things,
listening that is obedience,
trusting that is poverty,
loving that is chastity.

The vows we take
at the Spirit's leading
are seeds
that can grow in our hearts
into mighty trees
for the healing of nations.

God plants
but we must water
with prayer,
with faithfulness.
This way
joy
comes into the world.

Some things to think about and talk about

These are some Commandments
written by Dr. Kent Keith
when he was 19 years old,
a sophomore at Harvard College.
He wrote them in 1968
as part of a book
for student leaders
called
The Silent Revolution:
Dynamic Leadership in the Student Council.
Mother Teresa of Calcutta
put up a version of them
on the wall of Shishu Bhavan,

her children's home
in Calcutta, India:

The Paradoxical Commandments
People are illogical, unreasonable, and self-centered.
Love them anyway.
If you do good, people will accuse you of selfish ulterior motives.
Do good anyway.
If you are successful, you will win false friends and true enemies.
Succeed anyway.
The good you do today will be forgotten tomorrow.
Do good anyway.
Honesty and frankness make you vulnerable.
Be honest and frank anyway.
The biggest men and women with the biggest ideas
can be shot down by the smallest men and women
with the smallest minds.
Think big anyway.
People favor underdogs but follow only top dogs.
Fight for a few underdogs anyway.
What you spend years building may be destroyed overnight.
Build anyway.
People really need help but may attack you if you do help them.
Help people anyway.
Give the world the best you have and you'll get kicked in the teeth.
Give the world the best you have anyway. [33]

What kind of world
do you want to live in?

What do you think
God is saying to you?

What is your dream
for your life as a brother or sister?

What do you think you can do
with God's help

to make it come true?
Write it down.

Take a moment
to tell somebody what
you think about these things.

To Sum Up: Important Teachings to Remember from This Chapter

1. The vows help us help God
   to create a better world.
2. Prayer helps us to ask God for strength
   and grace in difficult times.
3. The example of other men and women
   in religious life can help us in our life.

Appendix

Universal Declaration of Human Rights [34]

PREAMBLE

Whereas recognition of the inherent dignity and of the equal and inalienable rights of all members of the human family is the foundation of freedom, justice and peace in the world,
Whereas disregard and contempt for human rights have resulted in barbarous acts which have outraged the conscience of mankind, and the advent of a world in which human beings shall enjoy freedom of speech and belief and freedom from fear and want has been proclaimed as the highest aspiration of the common people,
Whereas it is essential, if man is not to be compelled to have recourse, as a last resort, to rebellion against tyranny and oppression, that human rights should be protected by the rule of law,
Whereas it is essential to promote the development of friendly relations between nations,
Whereas the peoples of the United Nations have in the Charter reaffirmed their faith in fundamental human rights, in the dignity and worth of the human person and in the equal rights of men and women and have determined to promote social progress and better standards of life in larger freedom,
Whereas Member States have pledged themselves to achieve, in co-operation with the United Nations, the promotion of universal respect for and observance of human rights and fundamental freedoms,
Whereas a common understanding of these rights and freedoms is of the greatest importance for the full realization of this pledge,
Now, Therefore THE GENERAL ASSEMBLY proclaims THIS UNIVERSAL DECLARATION OF HUMAN RIGHTS as a common standard of achievement for all peoples and all nations, to the end that every individual and every organ of society, keeping this Declaration constantly in mind, shall strive by teaching and education to promote respect for these rights and freedoms

and by progressive measures, national and international, to secure their universal and effective recognition and observance, both among the peoples of Member States themselves and among the peoples of territories under their jurisdiction.

Article 1.
All human beings are born free and equal in dignity and rights. They are endowed with reason and conscience and should act towards one another in a spirit of brotherhood.

Article 2.
Everyone is entitled to all the rights and freedoms set forth in this Declaration, without distinction of any kind, such as race, colour, sex, language, religion, political or other opinion, national or social origin, property, birth or other status. Furthermore, no distinction shall be made on the basis of the political, jurisdictional or international status of the country or territory to which a person belongs, whether it be independent, trust, non-self-governing or under any other limitation of sovereignty.

Article 3.
Everyone has the right to life, liberty and security of person.

Article 4.
No one shall be held in slavery or servitude; slavery and the slave trade shall be prohibited in all their forms.

Article 5.
No one shall be subjected to torture or to cruel, inhuman or degrading treatment or punishment.

Article 6.
Everyone has the right to recognition everywhere as a person before the law.

Article 7.
All are equal before the law and are entitled without any discrimination to equal protection of the law. All are entitled to equal protection against any discrimination in violation of this Declaration and against any incitement to such discrimination.

Article 8.
Everyone has the right to an effective remedy by the competent national tribunals for acts violating the fundamental rights granted him by the constitution or by law.

Article 9.
No one shall be subjected to arbitrary arrest, detention or exile.

Article 10.
Everyone is entitled in full equality to a fair and public hearing by an independent and impartial tribunal, in the determination of his rights and obligations and of any criminal charge against him.

Article 11.
(1) Everyone charged with a penal offence has the right to be presumed innocent until proved guilty according to law in a public trial at which he has had all the guarantees necessary for his defence.
(2) No one shall be held guilty of any penal offence on account of any act or omission which did not constitute a penal offence, under national or international law, at the time when it was committed. Nor shall a heavier penalty be imposed than the one that was applicable at the time the penal offence was committed.

Article 12.
No one shall be subjected to arbitrary interference with his privacy, family, home or correspondence, nor to attacks upon his honor and reputation. Everyone has the right to the protection of the law against such interference or attacks.

Article 13.
(1) Everyone has the right to freedom of movement and residence within the borders of each state.
(2) Everyone has the right to leave any country, including his own, and to return to his country.

Article 14.
(1) Everyone has the right to seek and to enjoy in other countries asylum from persecution.
(2) This right may not be invoked in the case of prosecutions genuinely arising from non-political crimes or from acts contrary to the purposes and principles of the United Nations.

Article 15.
(1) Everyone has the right to a nationality.
(2) No one shall be arbitrarily deprived of his nationality nor denied the right to change his nationality.

Article 16.
(1) Men and women of full age, without any limitation due to race, nationality or religion, have the right to marry and to found a family. They are entitled to equal rights as to marriage, during marriage and at its dissolution.
(2) Marriage shall be entered into only with the free and full consent of the intending spouses.
(3) The family is the natural and fundamental group unit of society and is entitled to protection by society and the State.

Article 17.
(1) Everyone has the right to own property alone as well as in association with others.
(2) No one shall be arbitrarily deprived of his property.

Article 18.
Everyone has the right to freedom of thought, conscience and religion; this right includes freedom to change his religion or belief, and freedom, either alone or in community with others and in public or private, to manifest his religion or belief in teaching, practice, worship and observance.

Article 19.
Everyone has the right to freedom of opinion and expression; this right includes freedom to hold opinions without interference and to seek, receive and impart information and ideas through any media and regardless of frontiers.

Article 20.
(1) Everyone has the right to freedom of peaceful assembly and association.
(2) No one may be compelled to belong to an association.

Article 21.
(1) Everyone has the right to take part in the government of his country, directly or through freely chosen representatives.
(2) Everyone has the right of equal access to public service in his country.
(3) The will of the people shall be the basis of the authority of government; this will shall be expressed in periodic and genuine elections which shall be by universal and equal suffrage and shall be held by secret vote or by equivalent free voting procedures.

Article 22.
Everyone, as a member of society, has the right to social security and is entitled to realization, through national effort and international co-operation and in accordance with the organization and resources of each State, of the economic, social and cultural rights indispensable for his ignity and the free development of his personality.

Article 23.
(1) Everyone has the right to work, to free choice of employment, to just and favorable conditions of work and to protection against unemployment.
(2) Everyone, without any discrimination, has the right to equal pay for equal work.
(3) Everyone who works has the right to just and favorable remuneration ensuring for himself and his family an existence worthy of human dignity, and supplemented, if necessary, by other means of social protection.

(4) Everyone has the right to form and to join trade unions for the protection of his interests.

Article 24.
Everyone has the right to rest and leisure, including reasonable limitation of working hours and periodic holidays with pay.

Article 25.
(1) Everyone has the right to a standard of living adequate for the health and well-being of himself and of his family, including food, clothing, housing and medical care and necessary social services, and the right to security in the event of unemployment, sickness, disability, widowhood, old age or other lack of livelihood in circumstances beyond his control.
(2) Motherhood and childhood are entitled to special care and assistance. All children, whether born in or out of wedlock, shall enjoy the same social protection.

Article 26.
(1) Everyone has the right to education. Education shall be free, at least in the elementary and fundamental stages. Elementary education shall be compulsory. Technical and professional education shall be made generally available and higher education shall be equally accessible to all on the basis of merit.
(2) Education shall be directed to the full development of the human personality and to the strengthening of respect for human rights and fundamental freedoms. It shall promote understanding, tolerance and friendship among all nations, racial or religious groups, and shall further the activities of the United Nations for the maintenance of peace.
(3) Parents have a prior right to choose the kind of education that shall be given to their children.

Article 27.
(1) Everyone has the right freely to participate in the cultural life of the community, to enjoy the arts and to share in scientific advancement and its benefits.

(2) Everyone has the right to the protection of the moral and material interests resulting from any scientific, literary or artistic production of which he is the author.

Article 28.
Everyone is entitled to a social and international order in which the rights and freedoms set forth in this Declaration can be fully realized.

Article 29.
(1) Everyone has duties to the community in which alone the free and full development of his personality is possible.
(2) In the exercise of his rights and freedoms, everyone shall be subject only to such limitations as are determined by law solely for the purpose of securing due recognition and respect for the rights and freedoms of others and of meeting the just requirements of morality, public order and the general welfare in a democratic society.
(3) These rights and freedoms may in no case be exercised contrary to the purposes and principles of the United Nations.

Article 30.
Nothing in this Declaration may be interpreted as implying for any State, group or person any right to engage in any activity or to perform any act aimed at the destruction of any of the rights and freedoms set forth herein.

Endnotes

[1] Max Lucado, *The Applause of Heaven* (Nashville, Tenn.: Thomas Nelson, 2011).

[2] Dag Hammarskjöld, *Markings* (New York: Alfred A. Knopf, 1966).

[3] Peter Maurin, *Easy Essays* (Chicago: Franciscan Herald Press, 1984) 109.

[4] Anthony J. Gittens, CSSp, "Run Not Away, But Pursue!," *Religious Life Review* 51:274 (May/June 2012): 135-153.

[5] Petà Dunstan, email to author, April 4, 2012. Dr. Dunstan is the editor of the *Anglican Religious Communities Year Book*, 2012-13 (Norwich: Canterbury Press, 2012).

[6] Institute for Intercultural Studies, Margaret Meade; available at: http://www.interculturalstudies.org/faq.html#quote (accessed August 30, 2012). "We have been unable to locate when and where it was first cited…we believe it came into circulation through a newspaper report…it reflected a conviction that she expressed often, in different contexts and phrasings."

[7] "Constance, Nun, and Her Companions, commonly called 'The Martyrs of Memphis,' 1878," The Episcopal Church, conforming to General Convention 2009, *Holy Women, Holy Men, Celebrating The Saints* (New York: Church Publishing Company, 2010), 570.

[8] Richard Anthony Carter, *In Search of the Lost: The Death and Life of Seven Peacemakers of the Melanesian Brotherhood* (Norwich: Canterbury Press, 2006), 159-160.

[9] The Episcopal Church, *The Book of Common Prayer* (New York: The Church Hymnal Corporation, 1979), 125. The possessive pronoun "your" has been changed to proper noun

"God" to accommodate a shift from a prayer addressed to God to a description of our relationship to God.

[10] *The Book of Common Prayer*, 304-305. The possessive pronoun "your" has been changed to "our" to accommodate an editorial change from a question to a declaration of an obligation placed on all Baptized people.

[11] Mary Bosanquet, *The Life and Death of Dietrich Bonhoeffer* (London: Hodder and Stoughton Ltd, 1968) 277.

[12] Nuremberg Defense, Wikipedia; available at: http://en.wikipedia.org/wiki/superior_orders (accessed August 20, 2012). "This is a legal defense that essentially states that the defendant was "only following orders" ("Befehl ist Befehl," literally "an order is an order") and is therefore not responsible for his or her crimes. Before the ending of WWII, the Allies suspected such a defense might be employed, and issued the London Charter of the International Military Tribunal (IMT), which specifically stated that following an unlawful order is not a valid defense against charges of war crimes."

[13] *The Book of Common Prayer*, A Collect for Peace, 99. "You" has been changed to "God" to accommodate an editorial change from a statement addressed to God to a statement describing our relationship with God.

[14] H. A. Williams CR, *Poverty, Chastity and Obedience: The True Virtues* (London: Mitchell Beasley, 1975), 48.

[15] William J. Short, *Poverty and Joy: The Franciscan Tradition* (Maryknoll, NY: Orbis Books, 1999), 58.

[16] Short, *Poverty and Joy*, 31.

[17] Short, *Poverty and Joy*, 66-67.

[18] Short, *Poverty and Joy*, 59.

[19] Short, *Poverty and Joy*, 61.

[20] St. Ignatius of Loyola, Suscipe; available from: http://www.bc.edu/bc_org/prs/stign/prayers.html (accessed August 24, 2012).

[21] 2013 World Hunger and Poverty Facts and Statistics: available from: http://www.worldhunger.org/articles/Learn/world%20hunger%20facts%202002.htm#Does_the_world_produce_enough_to_feed_everyone (accessed June 22, 2012).

[22] Colin A. Carter and Henry I. Miller, "Corn for food, not fuel," *NY Times*, July 30, 2012; available from: http//www.nytimes.com/2012/07/31/opinion/corn-for-food-not-fuel.html (accessed December 17, 2013).

[23] The Abolition Project; available from: http://abolition.e2bn.org/people_24.html (accessed September 6, 2012).

[24] World Pension Forum, "Nelson Mandela and Desmond Tutu at 1994 World pension Forum Conference;" available from: http://www.youtube.com/watch?v=kvctrQBM9-o (accessed September 6, 2012).

[25] Evan Osnos, "The Burmese Spring," *The New Yorker*, August 6, 2012, 54.

[26] Stephanie Thérèse, SLG, "Reflections on the Vowed Life: Commitment through Celibacy," in Nicholas Stebbing, CR, ed., *Anglican Religious Life: A Well Kept Secret?* (Dublin: Dominican Publications, 2003), 91-108.

[27] H. A. Williams CR, *Poverty, Chastity and Obedience*, 66.

[28] The Third Order American Province, *The Principles of the Third Order, Day Four* (The Society of St. Francis, Autumn 1996).

[29] Jad Adams, "The Thrill of the Chaste: The Truth about Gandhi's Sex Life," *The Independent*, September 6, 2010; available from: http//www.independent.co.uk/arts-entertainment/books/features/thrill-of-the-chaste-the-truth-about-gandhis-sex-life-1937411.html (accessed December 17, 2013).

[30] Peter Block, Community: *The Structure of Belonging* (San Francisco: Berrett-Koehler, 2008), xi.

[31] Michael Lapsley with Stephen Karakashian, *Redeeming the Past: My Journey from Freedom Fighter to Healer* (Maryknoll, NY: Orbis Books, 2012), Preface, xi.

[32] Institute for Healing Memories; available from: http://www.healing-memories.org (accessed December 17, 2013).

[33] Kent M. Keith, *Paradoxical Commandments*; available from: http://www.kentmkeith.com/commandments.html (accessed August 26, 2012).

[34] United Nations General Assembly, *Universal Declaration of Human Rights*, December 10, 1948; available from: http://www.un.org/en/documents/udhr/index.shtml (accessed August 25, 2012).

Find a Religious Order near you:

Anglican Religious Communities
Index of Communities by Location
http://communities.anglicancommunion.org/communities/index.cfm?types+bylocation

Get more copies of *The Vows Book: Anglican Teaching on the Vows of Obedience, Poverty and Chastity* at www.Amazon.com

Learn more about Brother Clark Berge's ministry as Minister General for the Society of St. Francis and his reflections on life on his blog: "Itinerarium: The World is my Friary," which is available at:
www.brclarkberge.blogspot.com

Printed in Great Britain
by Amazon